PLANETARY  S O

Making Waves

SAVING OUR OCEAN

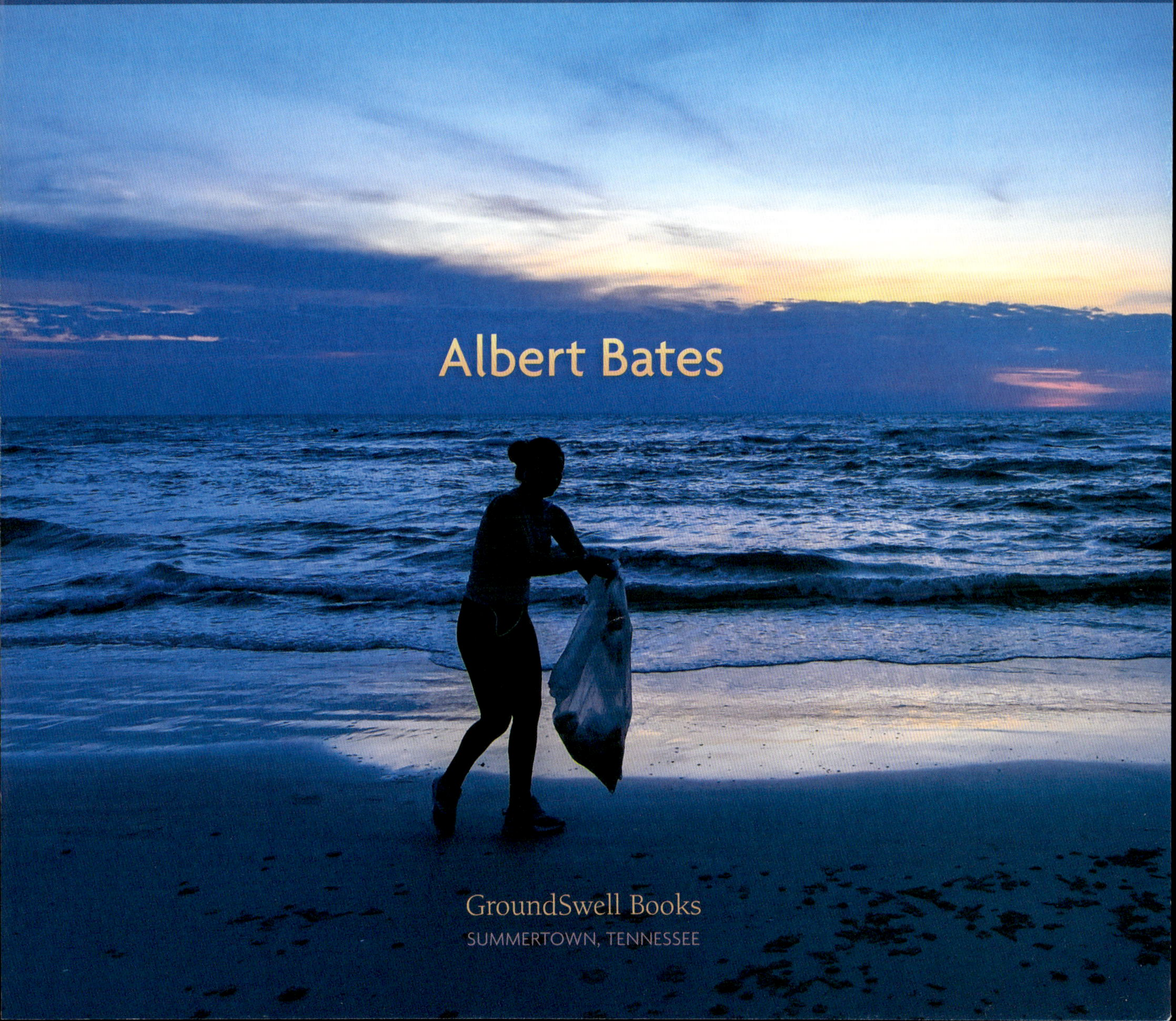

Albert Bates

GroundSwell Books
SUMMERTOWN, TENNESSEE

Library of Congress Cataloging-in-Publication Data available upon request.

 We chose to print this title on paper certified by The Forest Stewardship Council® (FSC®), a global, not-for-profit organization dedicated to the promotion of responsible forest management worldwide.

© 2021 Albert Bates

All rights reserved. No portion of this book may be reproduced by any means whatsoever, except for brief quotations in reviews, without written permission from the publisher.

Stock photography: 123 RF
Cover and interior design: John Wincek

Printed in China

GroundSwell Books
an imprint of Book Publishing Company
PO Box 99
Summertown, TN 38483
888-260-8458
bookpubco.com

ISBN: 978-1-939053-33-6

28 25 24 23 22 21   1 2 3 4 5 6 7 8 9

CONTENTS

INTRODUCTION   IV

CHAPTER 1: The Amazing Ocean We Depend On 1
The Balance of Ocean Life   3
The Ocean Food Pyramid   4
The Blue Acceleration   5
How We Use the Ocean   7

CHAPTER 2: The Ocean's Plight 9
Overfishing   9
Pollution   11
Radioactive Pollution   13
Noise Pollution   14
Combined Effects of Pollution   16

CHAPTER 3: Climate Change and the Ocean 19
Melting Ice   20
Sea Level Rise   22
Acid in the Ocean   24
More Frequent, Stronger Storms   25
Increased Salinity   27
The Loss of Coastal Vegetation   28

CHAPTER 4: Be an Emergency Planetary Technician 31
Allow the Ocean to Rebalance   32
Restore Marine Plants and Corals   33
Cleaning Up Our Act   35
What We All Can Do   37

CONCLUSION   38
INDEX   39

INTRODUCTION

Seventy percent of Earth's surface is water, and almost all of that is in the ocean. If you crossed the Pacific at its widest point, you'd travel through 13 time zones. Even though Earth's ocean is deeper than Mount Everest is tall, our ocean and watery atmosphere are still just a thin skin compared to the size of the planet. We call our planet's skin the biosphere.

The ocean was the source for all life on Earth. As simple sea organisms grew and reproduced, they rearranged the oxygen and nitrogen that filled our atmosphere, creating the ideal conditions for more complicated life forms in the sea and on land. Some of the world's oldest sea creatures—lobsters, crabs, millipedes, spiders, and some flying insects—still survive. Certain aquatic animals transformed from breathing through gills to developing lungs and so were able to emerge from the ocean and live on land.

Our blood is salty like the sea for a good reason. Blood is a private ocean that remembers what life was like for those microscopic organisms that dominated the first billions of years of life on Earth. The watery portion of blood, the plasma, has a concentration of salt and other ions that is remarkably similar to seawater.

Seawater is the circulatory system of our planet. When Earth gets a fever, her blood runs hot, and she responds by perspiring (casting off more heat into space and making more rain), taking deep breaths (absorbing more carbon dioxide and creating fiercer winds), and drinking more water (floods, melting ice, and supersized hurricanes).

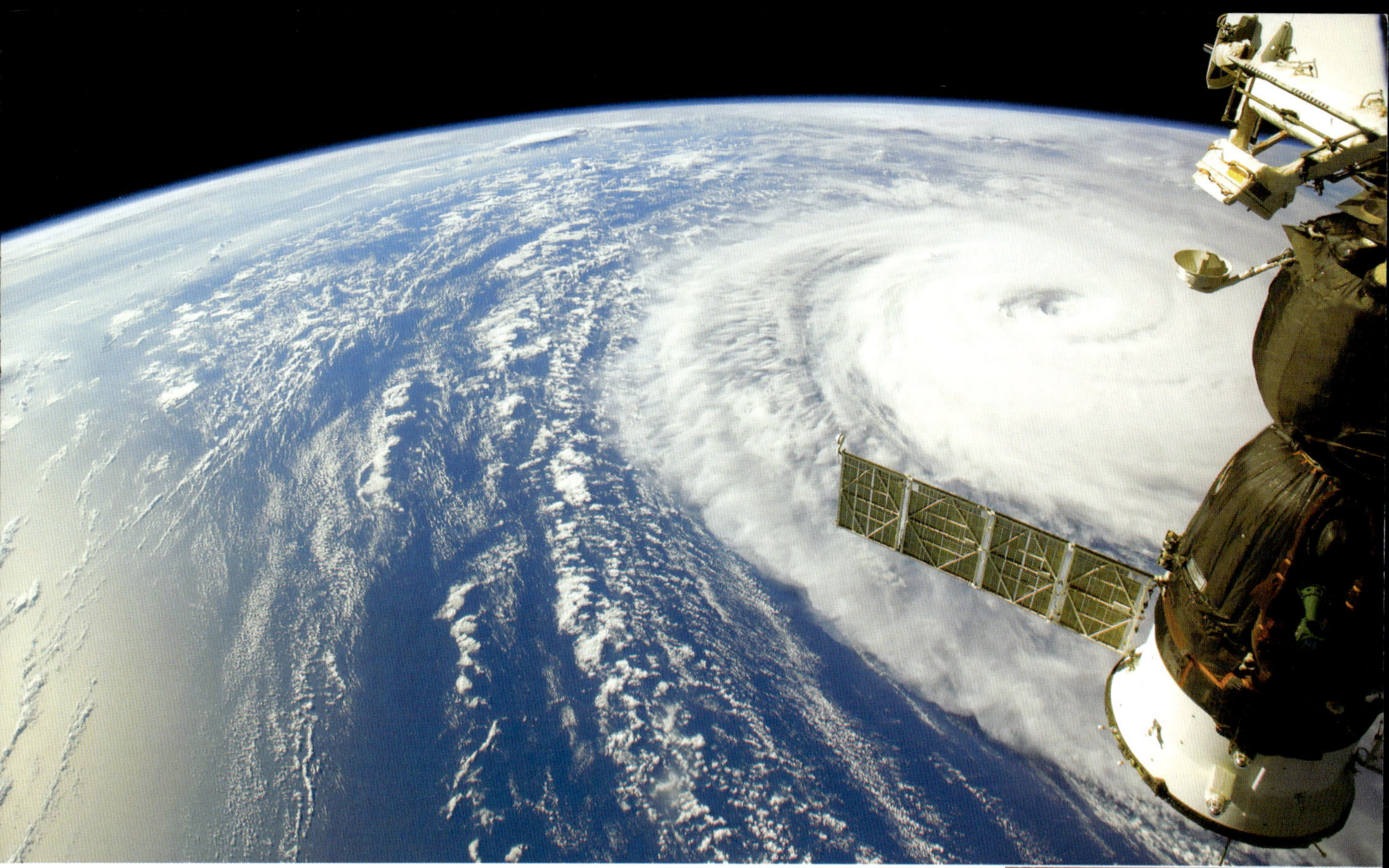

Not only is Earth fevering and the ocean responding to that fever, but also pollution from human activity and our overfishing of the seas are disrupting the diversity of life we land dwellers depend on. As we'll see in this book, that diversity not only feeds us but also plays a part in keeping our atmosphere comfortable so we can live.

Although we give names to separate areas of the ocean, there truly is just one ocean. What happens in one part of the ocean also affects it somewhere else. There are steps, big and small, that we can take to stop the destructive forces that are making the ocean unhealthy. Let's learn about how ocean environments work together; what's being done to create a cleaner, calmer ocean; and what each of us can do to make waves, in our own way, to bring about positive change.

CHAPTER 1

The Amazing Ocean We Depend On

Three main forces direct the movement of water in the ocean: waves, currents, and tides. The spin of the Earth, the push of winds, the rumbling of earthquakes and volcanoes, and the movement of landslides create waves. Most of the waves you see are the shorter, less intense variety that occurs at the surface, and, most of the time, those are caused by winds blowing across the water. More massive waves, such as tsunamis or tidal waves, are most often caused by underwater earthquakes and can bring considerable damage on land. The slope of the seafloor at the ocean's edge can determine whether waves will crash violently or gently curl.

 continuous stream of water moving along a definite path is called a current. It does not have to move horizontally along the surface; it could be a movement of water coming from a great depth

or shallow water sinking toward the ocean floor. Wind, tides, the density of the water, and the rotation of Earth are what drive currents. Warm water will rise above cold water, and because freshwater is less dense than salty water, it will rise while salty water sinks. Our planet rotates west to east. When ocean waters encounter a landmass in the Northern Hemisphere, they veer to the right, moving clockwise. In the Southern Hemisphere, they swerve left, moving counterclockwise.

Between Iceland and Greenland, salty meltwater leaving the Arctic moves southward and collides with warmer, fresher Atlantic coastal waters, creating the world's largest underwater waterfall. Equal to 2,000 Niagara Falls, this current plunges unseen down 11,500 feet (3,505 m)—three and a half times the drop of the world's highest terrestrial waterfall, Angel Falls in Venezuela—over a ridge called the Denmark Strait cataract.

The gravitational pull between Earth and the Moon causes tides—the rising and falling of the ocean in relation to land. The highest tides occur when the Moon is most full, which is when the water rises the most, but tides can change to high or low each day, or even more than once each day, depending on your location.

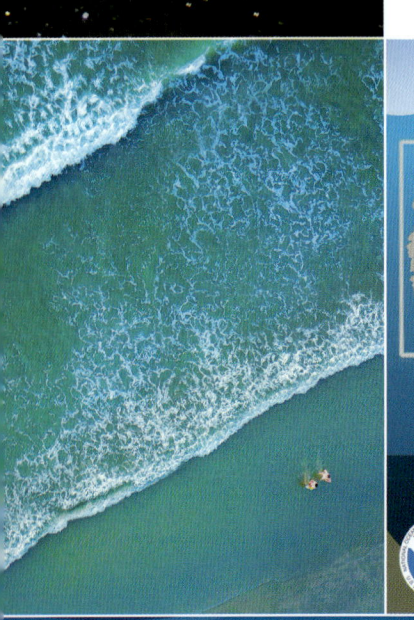

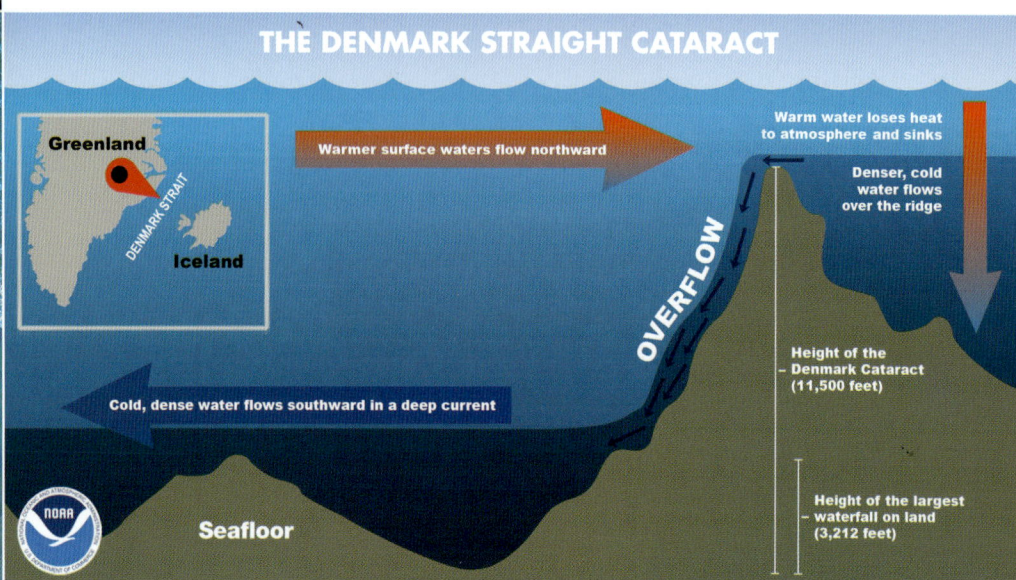

2 CHAPTER 1

The Balance of Ocean Life

Ecosystems consist of animals and plants that live in balance with each other and with their environment. Some aquatic ecosystems exist entirely in the ocean, while others have developed at the water's edge. Organisms within successful ecosystems feed each other and process each other's waste. Throughout evolution, these systems evolved to become very diverse and complex groupings of plants, animals, and microbes.

Keystone species are those upon which entire ecosystems rely. While every species is important to its ecosystem, if you take a keystone species away, the system can crumble. Marine animals form relationships with each other that help define their roles. Two organisms might have a predator/prey relationship, like a sea otter and a sea urchin, or they might have a friendlier sort of relationship called mutualism, such as when one fish will clean parasites from the teeth of another fish. No matter what the role, the loss of a predator or a beneficial organism can overturn the delicate balance of an ecosystem.

THE AMAZING OCEAN WE DEPEND ON 3

Ocean habitats vary a great deal, especially in their temperatures. Near polar regions, surface water temperatures go below freezing—about 28°F (-2°C)—but don't freeze because they are always moving. Warmer waters near the equator reach a temperature of 97°F (36°C), about the same temperature as your blood. The average surface temperature of the ocean is 63°F (17°C), but that is just at the surface, where the sun shines. The temperature decreases as we go deeper, beyond where sunlight can penetrate. The dark, cold zone known as the thermocline begins between 300 feet (90 m) and 1,300 feet (400 m) below the ocean's surface. All of these different areas—surface waters, thermocline, polar regions, tropical regions, deep water—create unique habitats for creatures that have adapted to them.

The Ocean Food Pyramid

The organisms in an ecosystem depend on each other for food—the energy they need to survive. The plantlike organisms found at the surface are called producers because they make their food by absorbing light from the sun and converting it into energy for other organisms in the ecosystem. Organisms living in deeper waters can't receive sunlight and must either rise toward the surface to eat or wait for food to drop down to them. Producer organisms that we can see with the naked eye include phytoplankton, algae, and seaweed.

Sea creatures that rely directly on producers for their food are called primary consumers. Corals, lobsters, and clams are primary consumers, and so are whales, sea turtles, and sharks. You can think of this as an energy pyramid, as large fish eat smaller fish, and in that

way the energy of the small fish is transferred to larger fish. Even decomposers, such as worms and bacteria that break down the dead and decaying material when producers and consumers die, are a part of this pyramid, feasting from all levels, top to bottom. The health of this pyramid food system is essential for the health of the ocean because all life in the sea is dependent on other life, just as life on land is dependent on the health of the ocean, as we shall see.

The Blue Acceleration

Since 2000, we have witnessed what is being called the "blue acceleration," a competition to claim and use ocean resources. The tremendous growth in this human activity has placed unprecedented pressure on marine ecosystems, which are experiencing overfishing, heatwaves, chemical changes in ocean water, and pollution from plastics and radioactivity.

The ocean has absorbed more than 90 percent of the heat humans have added to the Earth's system since the start of the Industrial Revolution in the late 1700s. The Arctic will experience ice-free summers sometime in the 2020s, a condition known as "blue ocean." Even if we were to bring greenhouse gases down to where they were 200 years ago, it would take thousands of years for the ice in Greenland and Antarctica to form again. In the meantime, a combination of all that melted polar ice—and the fact that cold water expands when it warms—means that the almost 2 billion people who live on or near a coastline (about 28 percent of the world's population) may have to relocate.

THE AMAZING OCEAN WE DEPEND ON   5

The ocean also plays a significant role in regulating climate and weather. That means we can anticipate increased marine heatwaves, coastal flooding, extreme tropical storms, and wildfires.

From dying coral reefs to sea level rise, entire marine ecosystems are rapidly changing. We can see many of these changes in newspaper headlines and scientific reports:

- Many pesticides and fertilizers and medicines used on animals end up in rivers, coastal waters, and the ocean, resulting in less oxygen in ocean waters and toxins that kill or maim marine plants and shellfish.
- Oil spills and nuclear spills pollute the ocean, although air pollution is responsible for almost one-third of the toxic contaminants entering the water.
- Factories discharge sewage and other runoff into the ocean, also killing marine plants and shellfish. In the US, sewage treatment plants discharge twice as much oil each year (from disposed engine oil or gas and oil washing from streets) as tanker spills or drilling disasters.
- Plastic items dumped by cruise ships, spilled from freighters, or making their way by land or river from factories and garbage dumps break down into tiny fragments called microplastics. The quantity of microplastics in the ocean will soon outweigh all the fish in the sea.

- Shipping and other human activities have caused the migration of countless plants and animals into coastal waters and have disrupted the ecological balance there.
- Many kinds of seafood are fished to the point that there are no longer enough of them to reproduce and maintain their populations, leading to fewer places to fish and fewer fish to catch.

How We Use the Ocean

According to ocean experts, these are some of the types of human activity that are competing with each other and often making increased demands on ocean resources:

- Fishing for human consumption
- Harvesting sea life for animal feed and supplements for humans
- Offshore oil drilling
- Deep-sea mining
- Converting saltwater to drinking water
- Removing ornamental fish and plants for sale in pet stores
- Scientific research
- Shipping
- Laying undersea pipelines and cables
- Tourism and recreation
- Development of coastal land
- Renewable energy projects, such as ocean-based wind turbines
- Waste disposal
- Conservation and regeneration
- National claims on ocean space
- Military navigation

THE AMAZING OCEAN WE DEPEND ON

CHAPTER 2

The Ocean's Plight

Two of the greatest challenges to the health of our ocean are overfishing and pollution. Some of the most damaging activity has happened in the last 50 years.

Overfishing

Billions of people depend on fish as a source of food and income. Seafood accounts for 17 percent of all animal protein consumed in the world, and an estimated 200 to 500 million jobs are directly or indirectly connected with fishing grounds in the ocean and fish farms along the coasts.

Prior to the 1990s, almost all commercial fishing was done sustainably. Today, the species that are most sought after are overfished to some degree, and each year, the number of overfished species rises. Modern high-tech fishing ships work 17 times harder to catch the same number of fish as a sailboat with rods, lines, and hooks could in the 1880s.

Every year, trawlers that tow nets in the deep ocean damage an area the size of Europe or America that's full of plants and animals at the bottom of the ocean.

Of course, humans are not the only animals to eat fish. When we catch fish, there are fewer fish to feed other fish, seabirds, seals, and polar bears. We eat so many of the best-tasting fish that their numbers dwindle, especially the smaller fish and other sea life that sustain large fish. As a result, we starve out the larger fish that need those staple foods.

After the fish are gone, where shall we turn? Rapid climate change is causing a noticeable loss of crops around the world, and this is particularly so for half of all countries that already experience food shortages.

Fish farms were created in part because people believed that raising fish commercially would save wild fish from the danger of extinction. However, some fish farms are stocked with young fish (called "fry") that are taken from the wild. Also, many kinds of desirable food fish are carnivores and must be fed wild fish; it takes many pounds of wild fish to produce a single pound of farmed fish. Fish in close quarters must often be fed antibiotics to prevent infection, and this can lead to the growth of bacteria that are resistant to antibiotics. Fish that escape fish farms can introduce parasites and pathogens that wild fish have no natural resistance to.

Pollution

Pollution from human activity has not only reduced the number of fish we can eat but has destroyed whole ecosystems as well. The greatest sources of pollution are fertilizers, sewage, pesticides, and waste from manufacturing and mining.

In 1960, there were 15 million tons (13.6 million MT) of plastic in the world. By 2020, we were adding 400 million tons (360 million MT) per year. The amount of plastic entering the ocean is doubling every five years, so unless production of plastics plummets, by 2050 the world will be adding 1.2 billion tons (1 billion MT) per year. Today there is 1 ton (.9 MT) of plastic in the ocean for every 3 tons (2.7 MT) of fish. By 2050 or sooner, there will be more plastic than fish.

When a 2015 expedition went to the deepest part of the ocean, the Mariana Trench in the western Pacific, and took sea life, such as crabs and shrimp, from the ocean floor to analyze, they discovered that even those had plastic in their diets. There are now microplastics found in one-third of all fish caught and examined. Microplastics have been shown to cross from the blood into the brain and affect behavior. Reports of fish stranded on beaches, their bellies filled with plastics, are becoming more common.

Many types of plastics are known to cause cancer, but we don't know how completely toxic they are or what kinds of new plastic are being introduced every year. For seabirds, whales, and fish that fill up their stomachs with indigestible plastic debris, or sea animals that get tangled in abandoned plastic nets, six-pack rings, or floating ropes and fabrics, we don't need to know how toxic plastics are. These victims will die of starvation and strangulation, unable to defend themselves.

Coral reefs provide food, coastal protection, and income for some 275 million people worldwide who live near the ocean's edge. However, these reefs are under stress from climate change, pollution, overfishing, and the billion plastic items ensnared in them—including diapers, tea bags, shopping bags, fishnets, bottle caps, and toothbrushes. This is as true in remote reefs as in those close to cities.

When corals come in contact with toxins and plastics, their risk of contracting disease rises from 4 percent to 89 percent. That is because corals have fragile tissues that can be cut and wounded, and those wounds are easily infected if they come in contact with poison or an item covered in all sorts of microorganisms. Plastics made of polypropylene—such as toothbrushes and bottle caps—can become covered with bacteria that are associated with a group of coral diseases known as white syndromes.

In 1979, disease suddenly wiped out nearly all the staghorn and elkhorn corals in the Caribbean, the types of coral you so often see in underwater photos. The outbreak was one of many that have collectively destroyed 80 percent of living corals in the Caribbean since that time.

12 CHAPTER 2

Radioactive Pollution

On March 11, 2011, an earthquake in the ocean near northern Japan generated a 46-foot-high (14 m) tsunami that swept over the seawall at the Fukushima nuclear plant and flooded four operating reactor buildings with seawater, knocking out the reactors and their emergency generators. The reactors shut down, and without generators, the plant operators could not cool their radioactive fuel. Within hours, three of the reactors melted and exploded, sending parts of their radioactive fuel into the sky, land, and ocean.

The end of the accident was not the end of the story. Cesium-137, a man-made radioactive isotope, is still flowing into the ocean every day from the damaged and leaking reactor cores. In March 2013, a fish caught near the Fukushima plant had 7,400 times the safe limit for cesium and could easily have killed anyone who ate it. By the end of 2014, cesium from Fukushima had been transported by currents in the North Pacific from Japan to the Gulf of Alaska, where it was found as deep as 1,300 feet (400 m).

To stop this assault on ocean life and our lives, the owner of the plant constructed more than 1,000 tanks over a period of five years to hold contaminated water away from the ocean. In September 2019, the Japanese government announced that more than 1 million tons (900,000 MT) were in storage, but that space would run out by the summer of 2022. Experts are urging the Japanese government to not rush to release this radioactive water until the nearby communities and countries that would be affected are consulted.

THE OCEAN'S PLIGHT

Noise Pollution

We tend to think of the undersea world as a quiet place, but apart from a few distant locations, it seldom is. Depending on where you are and the time of year, the ocean can be as noisy as any city street or rainforest jungle. Shrimp, fish, and marine mammals all use sound, sometimes beyond the audible range of human ears, as a type of sonar to locate objects in their surroundings. They keep in nearly constant communication with each other, and they navigate by listening to sounds of familiar coastlines and detecting both nearby predators and unwary prey.

Unfortunately, the activity of oil and gas exploration, as well as freighters and cruise ships, creates a disorienting amount of noise, especially for marine mammals. This noise increases levels of stress hormones and can disrupt the way these creatures feed and breed, as well as how they swim and vocalize.

> Oil companies use loud blasts of air directed at the ocean floor to measure how that air is reflected by various formations so they can create maps of these formations. The blasts can be 10,000 times louder than a nuclear explosion 500 yards (450 m) away. The US Navy is using a similar technology to map 80 percent of the ocean. Not only are whales, which navigate by sound, seriously disoriented by these blasts, but they (as well as dolphins) also can be killed by the force of the blasts.

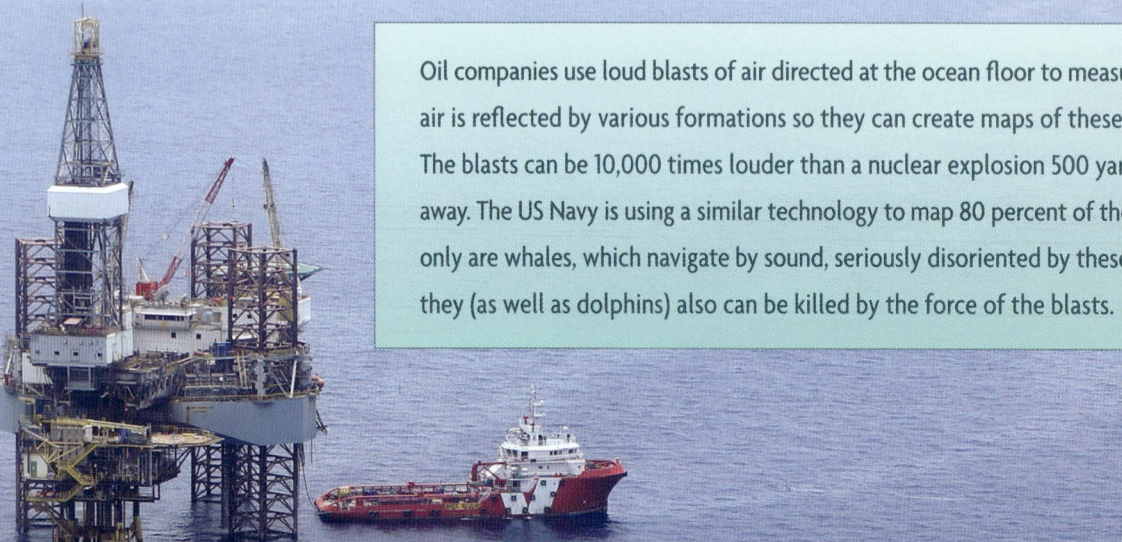

14 CHAPTER 2

There are many things we can do to prevent this kind of tragedy. Sadly, the most obvious action—prohibiting the use of sonar along whale migration routes—is often ignored. Other steps include slowing down ships that traverse the Arctic because a slower ship is a quieter ship. We can also keep away trawlers and cruise ships in seasons and regions that are important for mating, feeding, or migrating. And, banning exploration for oil and gas in order to slow climate change is long overdue.

Cruise lines offer relatively secure vacation travel, but the volume of waste these floating cities produce is large: sewage and solid waste, wastewater, oily bilge water, and air pollution. Each ship emits as much pollution as a small city, but that pollution is nearly unregulated and unpoliced. Cruise ships can emit as much air pollution as a million cars a day.

Each cruise ship passenger's carbon footprint (the amount of carbon their activity generates) is roughly three times what it would be for vacationers on land. Many ships shred their plastic to save space, but some take advantage of the difficulty in monitoring the presence of plastic particles in the ocean and discard their plastic along with treated sewage and gray water. Because cruise ships tend to concentrate their activities in specific coastal areas and visit the same ports, their cumulative impact on a locality can be significant.

THE OCEAN'S PLIGHT   15

Combined Effects of Pollution

Green and leatherback turtles are being driven to the brink of extinction by a combination of ingested plastics, toxic pollution, loss of breeding space, and disease. In 1988, half the harbor and gray seals in the North Sea (between England and Scandinavia) died from a distemper virus similar to that found in dogs. It took 22 years for the seal population to recover, but then it was struck a second time by the same virus, killing 20,000 North Sea seals. A parasite from domestic cat feces has attacked California sea otters, as well as clams and mussels, spinner dolphins, and beluga whales.

We know from experience that people who are stressed become more susceptible to disease because their immune systems become compromised. We see that bruised and broken corals do not heal quickly and that injured tissues of fish are much more readily infected than healthy ones. In much the same way, cumulative stresses compromise all life in the ocean.

THE OCEAN'S PLIGHT   17

CHAPTER 3

Climate Change and the Ocean

What are the effects of climate change on the ocean? The ocean can be a buffer against increasing amounts of greenhouse gases that lead to warmer temperatures, such as carbon dioxide (CO_2 and methane), by absorbing those gases from the atmosphere. In fact, 90 percent of all fossil fuel pollutants that enter the atmosphere every year end up in the ocean. However, there's a limit to what the ocean can absorb, and many scientists warn we are very close to that limit now.

The warmer that ocean water gets, the less carbon dioxide it can absorb. Not only is the ocean less able to buffer our warming atmosphere, but it also can lead to other effects that harm life on both the land and in the water due to those warmer ocean temperatures and increased carbon dioxide.

Melting Ice

When polar ice melts, it transforms the surface of the ocean from a mirror to a dark sponge. While a mirror would bounce away sunlight and leave its surface cool, a dark sponge absorbs it and warms. In this same way, when a warming ocean and atmosphere melt ice from the surface of the Arctic, Greenland, mountain glaciers, or Antarctica, they cause millions of square miles of the Earth's surface to switch from heat reflecting to heat absorbing. This speeds up the melting process, which increases the heat, which speeds up the melting.

More than 30 years ago, over 1,000 scientists warned the United Nations that unless we did something to reverse fossil fuel use, this ice-melting process could get out of control within 20 years. We didn't, and it did.

In the not too distant future, we expect ocean water to warm enough that the ice covering the Arctic will melt completely each summer. When it does, the sun's heat that is absorbed by exposed Arctic water

will increase ocean temperatures just as much as adding 25 years' worth of human greenhouse gas emissions in a single year. Even though we have not reached that point yet, the Arctic is already warming at a rate twice as fast as the rest of the planet, and it is warmer than it has been in 800,000 years.

When plants and animals die in the ocean, they sink to the seafloor and decompose, creating greenhouse gases. Right now, those gases are locked in the freezing polar waters. As the seafloor in that region warms, greenhouse gases will rise to the surface and add to our warming atmosphere.

The term "blue ocean event" refers to an ice-free Arctic when the ice melts in the summer, exposing the ocean's water.

Warming water also creates changes to the location and amount of nutrients for sea animals. Currents slow down when the difference between the water temperature at the poles and in the tropics decreases. Less mixing of ocean waters will bring fewer nutrients from deeper waters to the surface, reducing food sources for everything from algae to fish, seals, and turtles. Marine species that can swim are shifting toward cooler waters, but many stationary organisms, such as corals, have no way to escape from warmer, inhospitable waters and are left behind to wither and die.

Sea Level Rise

About 70 percent of Earth's freshwater is stored as ice in places such as Greenland, Antarctica, and the Himalayan mountains. Ice loss from Greenland is doubling every decade. At the other end of the world, in Antarctica, it is tripling. Melting glaciers from Alaska to Peru are sending rivers of water to the ocean.

Greenland ice is melting 7 times faster than it was 30 years ago, losing 370 billion tons (335 billion MT) to the sea every year. Since 1992, over 6 million people living along the coasts of the world have lost their homes from the water added to the ocean as Greenland melts. Another 250 million live barely 2 inches (5 cm) above the waterline.

Most sea level change does not occur in gradual steps, where each year, beachfront homes are a fraction of an inch closer to the water. Change comes in spurts; storms will combine with tides to push water toward land and make permanent changes to coastlines. Global warming of ocean water will cause higher storm surges and wind-made waves and will feed the strength of hurricanes and typhoons (the name for hurricanes that form in the Asian Pacific).

Miami Beach is now among the most flood-prone areas in the world. Any full moon can push water backward through the city's old storm drains and flood the streets and sidewalks. During a very high tide, Miami Beach has waves on its streets that are large enough to surf on! As the ocean rises, this will get worse each year, until the city disappears entirely and becomes an underwater attraction for scuba divers. Along with the city, Everglades National Park, a world biodiversity treasure, will also disappear.

Even the most optimistic projections predict that sea level rise will cause the type of coastal flooding in the tropics that usually happens every 100 years to occur every year by 2050. By the end of this century, it will be that extreme for most coastlines around the world.

CLIMATE CHANGE AND THE OCEAN

Acid in the Ocean

Since the start of industrialization in the 1700s, there has been widespread burning of fossil fuels and acres of land transformed from forests and meadows into farms and cities. All this activity has released more than 1,500 billion tons (1,400 billion MT) of carbon dioxide into the atmosphere; about half of that has been since 1950. The ocean absorbed about one-quarter of it, either dissolving it into seawater or having it washed into the sea by rivers or rainwater. Combining carbon dioxide and seawater produces carbonic acid. If you have ever had a fizzy drink, carbonic acid is where the fizz came from.

> Over the last 200 years, seawater has become 30 percent more acidic. At present rates, by 2060 seawater acidity could become 120 percent greater than in preindustrial times.

Plankton absorb the carbon from carbonic acid and combine it with sea salt to make the hard material for the outer shells and skeletons of sea animals. If they can't keep up with the rapidly changing amount of carbonic acid in the water, excess acid will start to dissolve seashells and corals, affecting clams, lobsters, shrimp, and oysters.

Too much acid in seawater also prevents coral-building organisms from building healthy reefs and may eventually destroy the reefs we already have. More than 30 percent of the world's coral reefs have died over the past 30 years, and 90 percent are projected to die by 2050—due to global warming, acidification, other forms of pollution, and overfishing. If carbon dioxide emissions are not curtailed, acidity is expected to rise 150 percent over the next 30 years.

> The coral colonies that build reefs and store carbon require clear water. Sedimentation from river runoff and manufacturing screens out sunlight and kills the polyps in coral colonies. After high temperatures, this is one of the principal causes of coral reefs bleaching and dying.

More Frequent, Stronger Storms

The ocean absorbs most of the heating effect of greenhouse gas pollution—90 percent of the excess heat on the planet—and it is changing the ocean significantly. Since the ocean's temperature was first taken with modern instruments half a century ago, the past 5 years are the top 5 warmest, and the past 10 years are also the top 10 years on record.

CLIMATE CHANGE AND THE OCEAN

Prior to 1980, there was very little warming below 1,000 feet (300 m), but now we see a warmer ocean at depths of 6,500 feet (2,000 m). This warming is irreversible on anything approaching human timescales.

As the ocean warms, heating also makes the atmosphere more unstable. As hot water evaporates, it moistens the air above the sea surface. In 2020, the air above the ocean held 5–15 percent more water vapor, on average, than it did in 1970. Storms grab that moisture to make more-powerful hurricanes and typhoons and cause more-extreme rains and flooding. We can also expect to see hurricanes forming much farther from the equator than they are now, so cities that might now only receive the remnants of hurricanes will eventually take direct hits. Hurricane season, which corresponds to the summer warming of the ocean, will also get longer, and the strength of hurricanes will become more deadly.

Already in India, the Middle East, and Australia, temperatures are pushing against the limits of human endurance. Rising temperatures are starting to limit the number of hours people can work, how much water is in the rivers, and whether food can be grown. In some places, even sleep is difficult.

26   CHAPTER 3

Increased Salinity

As chemicals from agriculture and other human activities drain into the ocean and certain greenhouse gases rain into the ocean, they increase the ocean's salinity, or its salt content. The saltier a body of water is, the less likely it is to absorb carbon dioxide from the atmosphere and the more likely it is to give it off.

We see this happening during ice ages. Lakes and rivers freeze, reducing the flow of fresh water into the ocean, and the ocean becomes saltier. This causes ocean water to release more carbon dioxide into the atmosphere, creating more of a greenhouse effect and rewarming the world.

These cycles of warming and cooling are a natural part of Earth's climate. However, the warming we're experiencing now is happening at an unprecedented rate that will disrupt plants, animals, and humans in ways that will make it difficult to change and adapt before significant losses are experienced.

CLIMATE CHANGE AND THE OCEAN   27

Kelp is a large brown seaweed that often grows up to 100 feet (30 m) tall. The plants grow together in what's called a kelp forest. Similar to a forest of trees on land, kelp forests are home to a variety of plants and animals that thrive in the habitats found at different levels. So, wherever there is kelp, there is an increase of fish, more oxygen held in the water, and lower acidity in that water. Kelp forests also keep coastal waters cool, and cool water can take the punch out of an oncoming storm.

Sadly, kelp forests are suffering from the impact of human activity, including climate change, overfishing, and overharvesting for food. (Did you know that kelp is used to make baked goods, medications, and even toothpaste?) In recent years, an explosion of sea urchins has decimated kelp forests, especially off the coasts of California and British Columbia. Sea life that fed on that kelp (and the animals that fed on that sea life, such as bald eagles and harbor seals) were also impacted. Fortunately, sea otters, the natural predators of sea urchins, are making a comeback, which will allow the kelp forests to regrow.

The Loss of Coastal Vegetation

Mangroves are small trees whose roots can survive in locations where freshwater flows into the ocean. The loss of coastal mangrove forests is especially tragic. The mangrove's sturdy root system reduces coastal erosion during severe storms and is the anchor for complete coastal ecosystems. These trees are extremely efficient at storing sources of carbon, piling up muddy sediments around their roots that are rich in nutrients. This allows mangroves and the many fish and crustaceans that live among them to reproduce and grow rapidly. When mangroves are removed to create new highways and urban developments, that carbon is no longer absorbed. The sediments decay, which sends carbon dioxide and methane (which also contains carbon) skyward.

Replanting and maintaining coastal vegetation helps ocean coasts adapt to warmer summers and colder winters, acting as a barrier against extreme storms while contributing to food security and biodiversity. Nearly 50 percent of coastal wetlands have been lost over the last 100 years as a result of the combined effects of development, sea level rise, warming, and extreme climate events.

Brian von Herzen is an ocean forester. Instead of growing trees from acorns, he grows kelp forests that pull nutrient-rich water from the deep and support favorable habitats for fish. In the future, he plans to expand these forests into the deep ocean using solar-powered robotics. The seaweed harvested from giant deepwater forests could be used for both fish and humans to consume—as well as to make biofertilizer, biodegradable plastics, and many other products.

CHAPTER 4

Be an Emergency Planetary Technician

I am an EPT: Emergency Planetary Technician. We've seen how the health of the ocean constitutes one of the planetary crises we now face. This chapter offers examples of emergency care that governments, companies, and you and I as individuals can provide. I believe that if many more people decide to join with me and become Emergency Planetary Technicians, we have a decent chance of restabilizing the ocean.

While some long-term changes can't be avoided, others are reversible if we act soon. If nations muster the will to cut emissions from fossil fuels to zero over the next few decades, that might give the ocean a breather. But there are also actions that can be taken to improve the quality of life in and around the ocean immediately.

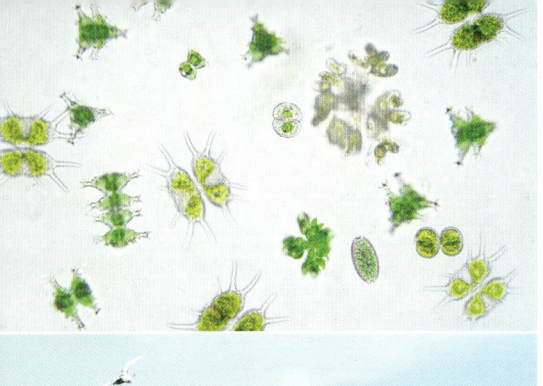

Allow the Ocean to Rebalance

There are basic changes that could be made that will help our ocean regenerate, providing cooler waters and increasing the oxygen and nutrients that would feed beneficial species. We could encourage the growth of kelp and mangrove forests, rebuild coral reefs, and acknowledge how having more whales would help reverse climate change.

Phytoplankton are tiny ocean algae that process carbon dioxide out of the atmosphere and release oxygen as a result. Phytoplankton are a favorite food of whales, and when a whale defecates, that excrement feeds the growth of more carbon-consuming phytoplankton. More whales lead to more whale poop, more phytoplankton, less carbon, and more oxygen.

If we had the same number of whales that existed before extensive whaling began—three to four times more than are alive today—it could significantly increase the amount of phytoplankton in the ocean and the carbon they capture each year. At a minimum, even a 1 percent increase in phytoplankton, thanks to whale activity, would capture hundreds of millions of tons of additional carbon dioxide a year, equivalent to the removal of millions of cars and the sudden appearance of 2 billion (1.81 billion MT) young trees.

Restore Marine Plants and Corals

Scientists have been experimenting with regrowing kelp forests on lightweight structures well offshore in 100 feet (30 m) of water. They believe that large grids of kelp planted this way will cool the shallower waters closer to land and favor the regrowth of edible seaweeds for the fish that forage on them.

Coral reefs provide the perfect natural shore protection, dispersing most of the energy of waves before it reaches land. As the waves pound on the reefs, coral sand is produced and transported to rapidly build beaches behind the reef. Because so many corals around the world are dying, tropical beaches that were growing until recently have begun eroding. Barrier islands are washing away, leaving coastlines more vulnerable to sea level rise and storms.

If the natural growth rates of coral can be significantly increased by providing more structures for corals to grow on—even with something like abandoned oil rigs or man-made rock created from ocean minerals—we could conceivably grow coral reefs faster than they are dying off and raise sandy coastlines faster than the ocean is rising.

Thomas Goreau is a marine biologist specializing in rebuilding coral reefs. He has been able to build miles of new or restored reefs in different parts of the world by using small amounts of electricity interacting with minerals in seawater to create a limestone base (he calls it biorock) that corals will attach to. Regenerated reefs can rebuild beaches and barrier islands more quickly than the rate of sea level rise, and those beaches provide a favorable location for trees to reestablish.

We can also protect shorelines by strengthening the natural vegetation (such as mangrove forests and ocean grasses) along those shores and by improving the water quality of the rivers that flow into the ocean. Restoration of river water can be accomplished by keeping erosion at bay—planting trees along the streams that feed into rivers—and by preventing the flow of trash (especially plastic trash) into the water.

Eden Reforestation Projects has helped to plant more than 335 million trees (many of them mangroves) in Madagascar, a large island off the coast of East Africa. Without these mangroves anchoring the shoreline, the island's soil had been washing out to sea.

Coastal vegetation pays huge dividends into the effort to reverse climate change by drawing carbon from the atmosphere during photosynthesis (the process by which plants "inhale" carbon and "exhale" oxygen). It also feeds and shelters many types of fish. To encourage the growth of coastal plant life, we need to stop constructing highways and buildings in areas where mangrove forests used to flourish and, where possible, restore those areas so those watery forests can regenerate.

Even if there is no further increase in carbon dioxide in the atmosphere, we are committed to sea level rise as much as 75 feet (23 m) from the excess carbon dioxide that is already there—unless it is rapidly reduced. No amount of emissions reduction, such as by switching to solar-powered automobiles or eating less meat, can reduce this excess. Only increased natural carbon sinks (such as plants that absorb carbon dioxide) can draw down these dangerous levels in time to avert extreme long-term changes that will last for hundreds of thousands to millions of years.

Cleaning Up Our Act

As we've seen, reducing pollution in coastal waters removes contaminants and excess nutrients that impair coastal ecosystems and, in that way, can help grow the capacity to withdraw carbon from the atmosphere and the ocean. Reduced pollution from shipping can also, to a limited extent, address the causes of climate change by keeping fossil fuels out of the atmosphere.

> Cargo ships that run on carbon-based fuels are causing damage to both the atmosphere and the ocean. Recognizing the problem, seafarers around the world have joined a movement to bring back sail transport. They may combine moving cargo with moving tourists or use their sailboats to stop at scenic port cities (such as those along the Mediterranean) or to pick up goods.

In 2017, the United Nations Environment Assembly adopted a global goal to stop the discharge of plastic into the sea. In 2018, at a meeting of the Commonwealth Clean Ocean Alliance in Vanuatu, 52 countries pledged to ban microbeads in rinse-off cosmetics and personal care products and to cut plastic bag use by 2021. With a fast-growing economy and a population of 1.3 billion, India struggles to manage its flow of waste and is a significant contributor to global ocean plastic. To help the problem, the Indian prime minister has announced his intent to eliminate all single-use plastic in the country by 2022.

The Ocean Cleanup, a nonprofit organization founded by Boyan Slat, a young Dutch engineer, uses another innovative solution to remove plastic from the ocean. In 2019, The Ocean Cleanup collected the first two shipping containers of trash from the Great Pacific Garbage Patch (an area of floating trash twice the size of Texas) by deploying surface traps along the path of ocean currents. As plastic wastes were driven by these currents toward their devices, the debris was gathered and moved to shore for recycling.

When The Ocean Cleanup learned that 1 percent of rivers are responsible for 80 percent of the plastic that reaches the ocean, they developed the Interceptor. This is a solar-powered device that can be placed in the mouth of a river to catch plastic before it reaches the ocean. The first Interceptors are now active in Indonesia and Malaysia and should be in all the heaviest-polluting rivers soon.

Plastic straws are one example of the most common and visible forms of plastic pollution. We use 360 billion of them each year and discard them when we're done. They end up in our waterways and across our shorelines. California became the first US state to implement a ban on plastic straws. A new company, Loliware, makes biodegradable kelp straws that add no flavor to either hot or cold drinks, outlast paper straws (which can wither only a third of the way through a drink, thereby requiring three straws for every drink), and can be reused if they are washed and dried.

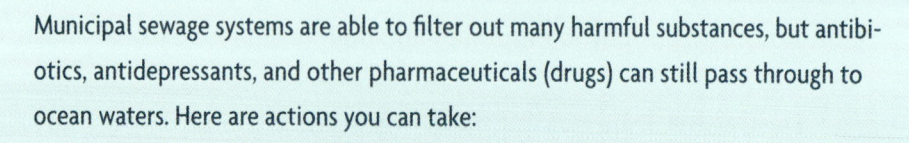

> Municipal sewage systems are able to filter out many harmful substances, but antibiotics, antidepressants, and other pharmaceuticals (drugs) can still pass through to ocean waters. Here are actions you can take:
>
> - Buy nontoxic sunscreens. Oxybenzone, a popular ingredient in sunscreens, is toxic to coral reefs, so be sure to check for brands that do not contain it.
>
> - Limit bulk purchases. Big bottles of unused pills create an opportunity for medications to end up in the water.
>
> - Use drug take-back programs. These programs allow people to drop off medications they no longer need at central locations, keeping unused drugs from being haphazardly discarded.

In January 2020, the nation of Palau became the first to ban reef-toxic sunscreens to save its corals. One of the side benefits is that those little plastic tubes of sunscreen that people use and discard will also vanish from Palau.

What We All Can Do

If we want to address the climate change and pollution that affect ocean health, we need to look closely at each of our individual lifestyle choices and identify areas where we could improve. The ocean we leave for future generations depends upon it.

Here are some "big picture" steps that local and national governments can take:

- Relocate populations back from vulnerable coasts.
- Build storm-resistant structures to protect ports.

These are steps we can all do to reverse climate change, create a cleaner ocean, and promote healthier ocean life:

- Eat less meat and less fish.
- Use energy less and more efficiently.
- Look for clothing made from natural, biodegradable fabrics, such as cotton and wool, instead of synthetics, and choose biodegradable plastics.
- Switch to shared transportation powered by renewable energy sources.
- Grow organic gardens to reduce the runoff from pesticides and insecticides.

BE AN EMERGENCY PLANETARY TECHNICIAN   37

CONCLUSION

By the time people born after 2010 become adults, they will already have witnessed many changes that would have astonished their parents. World population will have started to come down to a level that can be sustained ecologically. Food will be produced in many new and different ways, and none of those ways will harm the world. Wild animals will be expanding their range and numbers on land and in the sea.

All over the world, people will be trained to be Emergency Planetary Technicians and will be sent far and wide to arrest the spread of deserts, repair coral reefs, and restore wetlands. The destruction that had begun hundreds of years earlier will take a similar amount of time to undo, but the shift back to a healthy planet will have started.

The ocean is not merely the birthplace of life on Earth; it is what sustains us. The health and well-being of all of us depends on keeping the ocean happy.

INDEX

Page references for sidebars are in italics.

A

acidity of seawater, 24, 24–25, 28
air pollution, 6, 15
Alaska/Gulf of Alaska, 13, 22
Angel Falls (Venezuela), 2
Antarctica, 5, 20, 22
antibiotics, 10, 36
the Arctic, 2, 5, 15, 20–21
atmospheric warming, 19, 20, 21
Australia, rising temperatures and, 26

B

bacteria, 5, 10, 12
balance of ocean life, 3–4
biodegradable products, 29, 36, 37
biodiversity, 29
biofertilizer, 29
biorock, *33*
biosphere, iv
blood (human), as salty, iv
blue acceleration, 5–7
blue ocean, 5, *21*
British Columbia, kelp and, *28*

C

California, 16, 28, 36
cancer, plastics and, 12
carbon dioxide (CO_2)
    acidity of seawater and, 24, 25
    carbonic acid and, 24
    fossil fuels and, 24
    mangroves and, 28
    phytoplankton and, 32
    salinity and, 27
    sea level rise and, 34
    seawater circulatory system and, iv
    temperature and, 19
carbon footprint, *15*
carbonic acid, 24
the Caribbean, coral reef disease in, *12*
Cesium-137, 13
chemicals in ocean waters, 5, 27
climate, 6, 27, 29
climate change
    coral reef stress and, *12*
    food supply and, 10
    kelp and, *28*
    ocean as buffer against, 19
    oil/gas exploration and, 15
    reversing, 32, 34, 35, 37
CO_2 (carbon dioxide). *See* carbon dioxide (CO_2)
coastal areas
    coral reefs as protective to, 12
    cruise ships affecting, *15*
    development/population along, 5, 28, 37
    fish farms along, 9
    flooding/sea level rise and, 6, 22–23
    pollution reduction and, 35
    shipping/human activity affecting, 7
    vegetation and, 28–29, 33–34
    wetlands and, 28
Commonwealth Clean Ocean Alliance, 35
cooling/warming of Earth, 27, 28
coral/coral reefs
    blue ocean's effect on, 21
    carbonic acid and, 24, 25
    disease/stress and, *12, 17, 25*
    EPTs and, 38
    importance of, *12*
    as ocean health indicator, 6
    as primary consumer, 4
    restoring, 32, 33, *33*
    sunscreens and, *36, 37*
    toxins affecting, 12
cruise ships, pollution and, 6, 14, 15, *15*
currents, 1–2, 13, 21, 35

D

decomposers, 5
Denmark Strait cataract, 2
diseases, 12, *12*, 16, 17
dolphins, noise disorientation and, 14

E

earthquakes, 1, 13
ecosystems
    in balance of ocean life, 3
    blue acceleration and, 5
    changes in, 6–7
    coastal vegetation and, 28, 35

39

in food pyramid, 4
pollution and, 11
Eden Reforestation Projects, *34*
Emergency Planetary Technician (EPT), 31, 38
Everglades National Park, 23

F

fertilizers, 6, 11, *29*
fever of Earth, iv–v
fish
    antibiotics for, 10
    coastal vegetation as shelter for, 28, 34
    eating less, 37
    farmed, 9, 10
    fry (young), 10
    kelp and, 28, *29*, 33
    pollution and, 17
    radioactivity in, 13
    wild, 10
food production, 38
food pyramid, 4–5
food sources, water temperature and, 21
fossil fuels, as polluting, 19, 20, 24, 35
freshwater, 2, 22, 27, 28
Fukushima (Japan) nuclear explosion, 13

G

gas/oil exploration, as detrimental, 14, 15
global warming, 23, 25
Goreau, Thomas, 33
gravitational pull, tides and, 2
Great Pacific Garbage Patch, 35
greenhouse effect, 27
greenhouse gases, 5, 19, 21, 25, 27
Greenland, *2*, 5, 20, 22
Gulf of Alaska, radioactivity in, 13

H

health of Earth/ocean, 5, 9, 31, 37, 38
heat/heatwaves
    blue acceleration and, 5, 6
    fever of Earth and, iv
    greenhouse gases and, 25
    ice melting and, 20
    weather and, 26
Himalayan mountains, freshwater ice in, 22
human activity, as disruptive/demanding
    blue acceleration and, 5
    demands on ocean resources and, 7
    greenhouse gases and, 21
    kelp forests and, 28
    overfishing and, v, 5, 7
    pollution and, v, 5, 7, 11
    salinity of ocean and, 27
    shipping and, 7
hurricanes, iv, 23, 26

I

ice melting, iv, *2*, 5, 20–23
Iceland, *2*
India, 26, 35
Indonesia, Interceptor in, 36
Industrial Revolution, 5
Interceptor, 36

K

kelp, 28, *29*, 32, 33, 36
keystone species, 3

L

landslides, waves and, 1
life's origins from ocean, iv
lifestyle choices, 37
Loliware, 36

M

Madagascar, *34*
Malaysia, Interceptor in, 36
mangroves, 28, 32, 34, *34*
manufacturing waste, 11
Mariana Trench (Pacific Ocean), 11
marine animals, adverse effects on, 16, 21, 24, 28
medicines, 6, *36*
methane, 19, 28
Miami Beach, flooding and, 23
microplastics, 6, 11, 35
Middle East, rising temperatures and, 26
migration of species, 7, 15
mining waste, 11
the Moon, tides and, 2, 23
movement forces in ocean, 1
mutualism, 3

N

natural carbon sinks, 34
noise pollution, 14–15
nuclear spills, 6, 13

O

The Ocean Cleanup, 35–36
ocean resources, used by humans, 7
oil companies, air blasts used by, *14*
oil spills, 6
oil/gas exploration, as detrimental, 14, 15
overfishing
    about, 9–10
    blue acceleration and, 5
    coral reefs and, *12*, 25
    as demanding/disruptive, v, 7
    kelp forests and, 28
overharvesting of food, 28

Oxybenzone, *36*
oxygen, iv, 6, 32, 34

P

Pacific Ocean, iv, 11, 13, 23, 35
Palau, sunscreens and, *37*
Peru, ice melt and, 22
pesticides, 6, 11, 37
photosynthesis, 34
phytoplankton, 4, 32
plankton, 24
plastics, as pollutant
    about, 11–12
    blue acceleration and, 5
    cleaning up, 35–36
    coastal vegetation and, 34
    coral reefs and, 12, *12*
    cruise ships and, *15*
    extinction of turtles and, 16
    microplastics, 6, 11, 35
    plastic straws, 36
pollution. *See also* specific types of
    about, 11–12
    blue acceleration and, 5, 6
    combined effects of, 16
    coral reefs and, *12*, 25
    as disruptive, v, 9
    lifestyle and, 37
predator/prey relationships, 3
primary consumers, 4–5
producers, 4
pyramid food system, 4–5

R

radioactivity, 5, 13
renewable energy, 7, 37
restabilization/rebalancing of ocean, 31–32

rotation (spin) of Earth, 1, 2

S

sail transportation of cargo, 35
salinity of ocean water, 27
sea level rise, 6, 22–23, 28, 34
sea urchins, kelp and, 28
seafloor, 1, 2, 11, *14,* 21
seafood, as consumed, 9, 10
seawater, as circulatory system, iv–v
seaweed, *28*, 33
sewage, 6, 11, *15,* 36
shells of sea animals, carbonic acid and, 24
shipping activity, as detrimental
    commercial fishing ships, 9
    cruise ships, 6, 14, 15, *15*
    migration of species and, 7
    pollution and, 6, 14, 15, 35, *35*
Slat, Boyan, 35
solar-powered robotics, 28
sonar, used by marine animals, 14, *14,* 15
sponge effect in ocean, 20
storms, 23, 26, 28, 29, 33
stress hormones, in marine animals, 14
sunlight, 4, 20, 25
sunscreens, coral and, 36
sustainable fishing, 9

T

temperature of ocean water
    atmosphere affected by, 26
    climate/weather and, 5, 23
    currents and, 2, *2*
    greenhouse gases and, 19, 25
    habitats and, 4

    ice melting and, 21
    kelp and, *28*
    rebalancing and, 32
    records of, 25–26
tidal waves, 1
tides, 1, 2, 23
toxins, 6, 12. *See also* specific types of
tropical storms, 6
tsunamis, 1, 13
turtle extinction, pollution and, 26
typhoons, 23, 26

U

United Nations, 20, 35
US Navy, *14*

V

Vanuatu, ocean alliance meeting in, 35
volcanoes, 1
von Herzen, Brian, 28

W

warming/cooling of Earth, 27, 28
water density, 2
waterfalls, 2
waves, 1, 23, 33
weather, 6, 23, 26
whales
    pollution and, 12, *14,* 15, 16
    as primary consumers, 4
    rebalance of ocean and, 32
white syndromes (coral diseases), 12
wildfires, 6
wind, 1, 2
world population, sustainability and, 38

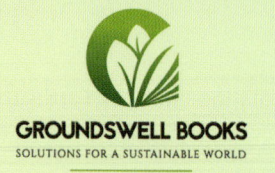

GROUNDSWELL BOOKS
SOLUTIONS FOR A SUSTAINABLE WORLD

For more books that inspire readers to create a healthy, sustainable planet for future generations, visit BookPubCo.com

Our planet's environmental problems have reached the crisis level. In response, we developed two vital series to help educate, empower, and motivate everyone to take action.

PLANET IN CRISIS SERIES

Addresses urgent challenges of climate change by focusing on specific issues, identifying their impact, and illustrating creative solutions that can make a difference.

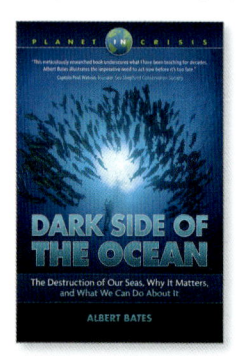

Dark Side of the Ocean
Albert Bates
978-1-57067-394-8 • $12.95

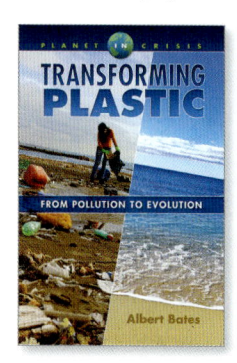

Transforming Plastic
Albert Bates
978-1-57067-371-9 • $9.95

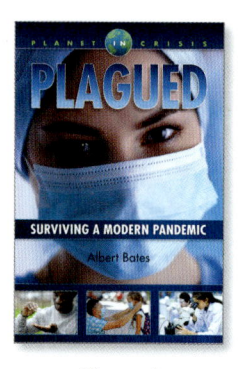

Plagued
Albert Bates
978-1-57067-400-6 • $9.95

PLANETARY SOLUTIONS SERIES

Inspiring young people to understand, challenge, and solve the environmental problems that put the Earth at risk.

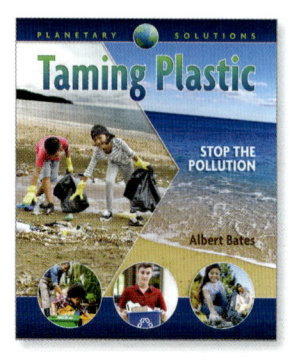

Taming Plastic
Albert Bates
978-1-939053-24-4 • $14.95

Purchase these titles from your favorite book source or buy them directly from:
Book Publishing Company • PO Box 99 • Summertown, TN 38483 • 1-888-260-8458

Free shipping and handling on all orders